THE DETERMINANTS OF PRICES OF NEWBUILDING IN THE VERY LARGE CRUDE CARRIERS (VLCC) SECTOR

Mustafa Nejem

DECLARATION

I hereby declare that the work reported in this dissertation is completely my own work unless otherwise stated, and that it has not been submitted previously for any award or degree at any other institute

_____   (Signature of Candidate)

_____   (Date)

Word count: 10. 500

ABSTRACT

The aim of the proposed research study will be to identify and analyze the determinants of prices of newbuilding vessels in the Very Large Crude Carriers (VLCC) Sector. Historical quantitative data was collected from Clarksons Shipping Intelligence Network (SIN) for the time period 2000-2018 about factors that academic literature defines as factors that could influence prices of newbuilding vessels in general and newbuilding VLCCs in specific, namely prices of second –hand vessels, earnings of VLCCs, sales in the sector, deadweight (DWT), scrap prices and freight rates. Data was statistically analyzed with SPSS. Descriptive statistics were calculated, while regression analysis was also held. Based on the findings of the research, prices of new built VLCCs were increasing after 2002 and until 2008. Then, a significant drop was observed in 2009. After that point in time, the price of new-built VLCCs has been declining, with a slight increase being observed from 2017 to 2018. Prices of second hand vessels followed the path of prices of newbuilding VLCCs over the review period, while it is worth noting that in 2014 and 2015, the price of second hand VLCCs increased, a trend that was not identified in the case of newbuilding ones. Earnings per day for VLCCs were significantly fluctuated over the review period. Ship owners of VLCCs saw their revenues reaching their lowest point in the review period in the end of the period in 2018. Demand for VLCC-seaborne trade in a global context was steadily increasing from 2008 to 2018, with a slight fluctuation being observed in 2009, when demand slightly fell, before it starts increasing again from 2010 and on. Following the path of demand, supply of VLCCs was also steadily increasing from 2000 to 2018. The scrap price at which VLCC were sold during the review period fluctuated to a considerable extent. Scrap prices for VLCCs reached their peak in 2010, before starting falling until 2016, while, after a short increase in 2017, VLCC scrap prices fell again in 2018. Freight rates also fluctuated considerably during the review period. In particular, after dropping in 2002, freight rates started increasing, reaching their peak in 2008, before significantly dropping until 2013. Research findings imply that the price of newly-built VLCC is determined by numerous factors, following the corresponding trends regarding the factors that influence prices of ships in general. Further, research findings indicate that supply and demand are important determinants of ship-owners' decisions regarding the acquisition of VLCCs, but not at what prices such decisions shall be made. It follows from the above that ship owners shall monitor the developments in prices of second-hand vessels, scrap prices and freight rates, in order to have a rough estimation of how prices of newbuilding shall evolve over time and make their ship acquisition decisions, while in such decisions they shall also take into account their earnings per day. Future researchers shall conduct the same research for wider time periods and for all other shipping sectors. as a means of identifying whether the trends and factors determining the VLCC sector are identified in other shipping sectors as well.

Keywords: Very Large Crude Carriers (VLCC), shipping industry, newbuilding vessels, supply and demand, freight rates

TABLE OF CONTENT

Chapter 1
INTRODUCTION

1.1. Research Aims and Objectives

The aim of this research study is to identify and analyze the determinants of prices of newbuilding vessels in the Very Large Crude Carriers (VLCC) Sector. More specifically, the proposed research study had the following objectives:

- To identify the factors that determine the prices of newbuilding vessels in the VLCC sector
- To examine whether these factors are consistent with those that academic literature suggests as factors that determine the price of newbuilding vessels in the shipping industry in general
- To comment on whether the fact that many VLCC have been scrapped shall be attributed to any of the factors considering supply, demand and prices of such vessels, or only to the fact that they tend to be substituted with ULCCs
- To provide implications for ship owners, as far as their vessel-acquisition decisions for VLCC are concerned

1.2. Research Background

The global shipping industry is highly vulnerable to external factors, while its elements are interrelated with each other and one affects the other (Branch, 2007). Since the start of the global economic crisis in 2009, shipping companies have switched towards the acquisition and operation of very large vessels, as a means of controlling their operating costs. Indeed, the main advantage that such very large vessels offer is the advantage of economies of scale, which reduces the cost per unit transported, while at the same time also reducing the energy consumed per unit transported, which is another front-burner issue that shipping companies and international shipping authorities have to deal with over the last decades (Tai & Wang, 2022). On the other hand, of course, the cost of acquiring very large vessels is by far higher, while at the same time shipping companies need to ensure that their very large vessels achieve full capacity at all times, in order to enjoy the – economic at least – advantages of operating these vessels (Stopford, 2009).

1.3. Research Rationale

In the context that shipping companies have switched towards operating very large vessels, it is very important to understand the price structure of such vessels, namely the factors that determine their price. Acknowledging and understanding such factors is very important for shipping companies, in order to design their vessel-acquisition strategies. In other words, by monitoring how specific factors and variables develop, ship owners shall be in a position to forecast – at least to the point that a forecast is always possible – when prices of very large carriers shall increase or decline, thereby also deciding when and how many vessels to order, as part of their overall commercial and business strategy. There are factors such as prices of second –hand vessels, earnings of VLCCs, sales in the sector, deadweight (DWT), scrap prices and freight rates, which are common factors that prices of newbuilding in general are said to be determined by (Stopford, 2009). Given that very large vessels are relatively new in the global shipping market, it was considered as interesting and important for ship owners of such vessels to identify and understand whether the market of very large vessels are driven by the same factors as other shipping sectors, for which more historical data is available. The particular sector of very large crude carriers (VLCC) will be used as a case study, given that very large containerships are fewer and newer in the market, so not much historical data is available.

1.4. Structure of Research Study

Chapter 2 reviews the existing literature on the subject under research. Chapter 3 outlines the methodology of the study, justifying the selection of specific research methods. Chapter 4 presents the results of the research, which are then discussed in Chapter 5 with respect to research aims and objectives and the theoretical framework developed in Chapter 2. Finally, Chapter 6 summarizes the main findings of the research, provides implications and conclusions for them, while also providing implications for future research.

Chapter 2
LITERATURE REVIEW

2.1. Very Large Crude Carriers (VLCC) and their Market

Very Large Crude Carriers (VLCC) are oil tankers with a DWT carrying capacity between 180,000 to 320,000 tons. This very large DWT capacity is the reason for which such vessels are also referred to as supertankers. VLCC have dimensions of 470m in length, beam of up to 60 m and draught of up to 20m. They have the ability to pass through the Suez Canal, while their operation is mainly concentrated in North Sea, Mediterranean and West Africa (Karan, 2022).

There are numerous benefits that megaships such as VLCCs are subject to. More specifically, through the acquisition and operation of megaships, ship owners enjoy high economies of scale. Obviously, the larger a vessel is, the higher carrying capacity it has, which means that megaships have the ability to carry bigger cargo volumes, thereby increasing their revenues per voyage, while at the same time also reducing the cost per unit transported. This, in turn, could lead to either enjoying higher profitability, or offering lower transportation costs for shippers, thereby also adding to the competitive advantage of shipping companies and charterers owning and operating such ships (Cullinane & Khanna, 2000). In the same sense, megaships could also be characterized as more energy efficient, in the sense that they help shipping companies in performing fewer voyages than required in the past for transporting the same volumes of cargo. This means that CO_2 emissions of ships are also reduced, which is very important for enhancing higher sustainability in shipping, if it is taken into account that CO_2 emissions from shipping operations form one of the most important factors contributing to the greenhouse effect and global warming, which form the mirror of global climate change (Zrinc, Oguamanam, Bosnjak et al., 2006).

However, VLCCs and megaships in general are also subject to important disadvantages as well. First and foremost, such very large vessels cannot be served by all ports of the world, because their sixe is such that not all ports have the necessary size and facilities to accommodate them. This means that shipping companies owning and operating such ships do not have the ability to benefit from lower port charges and less port traffic that can be found in less minor ports in a global context (Cariou, 2008). To make matters worse, it is their very large size that does not enable such ships to pass through some major sea passages, thereby constituting their voyages as lasting longer. This in turn undermines their commercial attractiveness, while at the same time also potentially adding to their operating costs per voyage. In addition to the above, VLCCs and megaships in general are difficult to navigate, which means that they require the occupation of the not so many available very experienced masters and seafarers all over the world. Last but not least, as also obvious, bigger vessels, such as VLCCs, are more expensive than smaller ones. This means that ship owners need to invest more money, in order to expand their fleet, which in turn means that they shall make bigger financial openings, not knowing exactly whether economic and overall shipping circumstances shall be as expected, when they get delivered their new vessels, approximately after three years from the placement of their order (Chen & Zhang, 2008).

The shipping industry in general, as well as the VLCC sector in specific, were highly affected by the global economic crisis that started in 2009 and its influence in global economic is still evident today. It is worth noting that freight rates collapsed by 85% within a period of five months after the start of the crisis, with the result that dry cargo ships, as well as tankers, could not even cover their operating costs. The tragedy of the situation was confirmed by reality, when several ship owners began to Withdraw their ships from the market and others scaled back to very large extent their investments in new shipyards. As a culmination came the inability of banks of the world to finance shipping companies, making things even more tragic, leading many shipping companies to even shut down their operations (Sanchez & Pérez Salas, 2009). Indicatively, in 2012 four effects emerged that further aggravated the situation in the shipping market. Bankruptcies, the reduced number of new orders, the large number of cancellations and at times the increased number of dismantling are the blows that hit the sector hardest. Further to the above, large and healthy companies, as soon as they realized that freight rates in a certain area showed increasing trends, "dropped" ships in these areas, in order to keep freight rates low. The reason they have been doing this is to cause further financial strain on small or ailing companies to prepare the ground for mergers and acquisitions (Hung & Chuang, 2012).

As Market Watch (2023) analyzes, the VLCC sector was highly affected by the COVID-19 pandemic and the Russian war in Ukraine as well, with the value of the market reaching USD 158,750 million in 2022. The market is expected to report an average annual growth rate of 2.3% in the next years (CAGR for the period 2008-2018 was 2,76%), to reach value of USD 182,220 million in 2028. In terms of freight rates, an increase of 21.5% was reported in December 2021, compared with December 2020, when almost the whole world was in a lockdown mode. By the end of December 2022, freight rates in the VLCC sector significantly increased. mainly as a result of very increasing demand all over the world, also boosted by the ban on Russian oil exports (Bertzeletou, 2022).

Based on the analysis provided by Maritime Executive (2021), ship owners are keen on demolishing their older and smaller ships, in order to purchase newer, more efficient and larger ones. Although VLCCs are very large ships, there is also the trend of ship owners to substitute them with Ultra Large Crude Carriers (ULCCs). Despite this trend, ship owners have been highly reluctant in selling their VLCCs for scrap after 2021, regardless of the fact that scrap prices for these vessels have climbed high since 2021, especially in the Indian market, and despite the fact that freight rates in 2021 were not so high, if the consequences of the COVID-19 pandemic are also taken into consideration. The main reason for this is that VLCCs offer ship owners high earnings and profits potential, so, taking into account the growing demand for seaborne trade, they believe that it is better to maintain them in their fleet. Further, the high earnings that ship owners have been subject to over the last 20 years from VLCCs have enabled them to have built adequate cash reserves. As such, it is not so urgent for them to earn cash through demolishing their ships, no matter if they are older than they should. Another reason has been the high prices of second-hand vessels, which has given the incentive to owners of older VLCCs to sell them in the second-hand market, rather than abolish them and sell them for scrap.

2.2.   Factors Affecting Prices of Newbuilding Vessels

Academic literature occupied with the shipping industry and maritime economics in general has identified a number of factors affecting prices of newbuilding. First and foremost, prices of newbuilding vessels are determined by sales volumes, i.e. demand for seaborne trade. Obviously, when demand for seaborne trade is high, ship owners tend to order more vessels, in order to benefit for this increase in demand. In such periods of high demand for vessels, their price increases, since ship owners are willing to pay more to acquire vessels that will help them in increasing their sales potential (Stopford, 2009). Based on the research findings of Michail (2000), demand for seaborne trade is undoubtly determined by GDP growth in a global context, due to the global nature of the shipping industry. Normally, when global economy performs well, this leads to an increased demand for industrial activities, which in turn leads to an increased demand for seaborne trade or goods and commodities that are used as raw materials or ready products in such activities. However, there are also the research findings of Adland & Koekebakker (2007), based on which demand for seaborne trade increases, when GDP growth diminished, the rationale behind this finding being that when GDP growth in a global context is low, this means that the global economy is either at a stage of decline or at an introductory stage. This means that sooner or later global economy shall enter the stages of introduction or growth, which means that demand for seaborne trade shall be expected to increase again, giving the incentive to ship owners to invest in the acquisition of new ships. No matter which of the two comes true, demand for newbuilding increases and so do their prices.

Prices of newbuilding are also determined by sales revenues, which in turn are also determined by freight rates. In short, when freight rates are high, earnings of vessels are also high, which adds to the willingness of ship owners to expand their fleet to gain higher revenues, thereby again creating higher demand for vessels, which in turn increases their prices (Cullinane, 2011). The analysis and research finding of Kou & Luo (2015) are very important in this domain, based on which ship owners take their ship acquisition decisions for newbuilding not based on freight rates in the short-run, but rather freight rates' forecast for the long-run. Based on the same research findings, opportunistic thoughts of ship owners to benefit for increased demand for seaborne trade and increased freight rates in the short-run lead to an increase in demand for prices of second-hand vessels, since this is the type of vessels that ship owners switch to, when they wish to take immediate advantage of current demand and freight circumstances. As for newbuilding prices, they are more elastic to long-run forecasts and fluctuations of freight rates.

Of course, it is not only demand that affects the price of newbuilding vessels, but also supply, expressed as the available DWT in a market. Based on basic economic theory, an increase in supply of goods leads to a decrease in their prices, while at the same time demand also increases. To put it differently, a shortage in supply of vessels, or when their supply is not enough to cover demand, shall lead to an increase in prices of vessels, and vice versa (Grammenos, 2013). The above are also verified by the analysis and findings of Adland, Norland & Sætrevik (2017). Based on these, when demand for vessels is higher than their supply, then prices go up, until some ship owners decide to drop out from their requests for new ship and the market comes closer to its equilibrium. In contrast, when there are not so many orders in shipyards, prices of new ships normally follow, until new ship owners place new orders and demand in shipyards starts increasing again.

Further, prices of newbuilding vessels are highly determined by prices of second-hand vessels. In particular, when prices of second-hand vessels are high, newbuilding vessels' prices are also high, as a means of maintaining the balance between the two. On the contrary, when prices of second-hand vessels are low, then the price of newbuilding vessels also decrease, in order for shipyards to give the incentive to ship owners to purchase new vessels, instead of switching to second-hand ones (Talley, 2012). The above relationship between prices of newbuilding and second-hand vessels also depends on the stage of the shipping cycle the shipping industry is, at the time ship owners make their ship-acquisition decisions. In brief, at stages of growth and maturity, when demand for seaborne trade is normally high, ship owners tend to switch to second-hand vessels, in order to take advantage of high demand as soon as possible – it takes about three years for newbuilding vessels to be delivered. At such stages, it is normal that prices of second-hand vessels become higher. At such circumstances, though, it is likely that prices of newbuilding do not decrease at the same extent as prices of second-hand vessels. This is because shipyards anticipate that ship owners will switch to second-hand vessels, so they offer more competitive prices, in order to persuade those ship owners believing that the stages of growth and maturity shall be bigger to invest in the acquisition of newer and more efficient vessels (Stopford, 2009). Last but not least, scrap prices are also important determinants of price of new vessels. When scrap prices are high, ship owners find it more attractive to demolish their older ships and purchase new ones, this increase in demand also leading to increase in prices of new vessels (Stopford, 2009). Ship demolition, which forms one of the main shipping markets, is indeed a major determinant of prices of new ships, in combination of course with demand and supply of vessels, as well as the stage of the shipping cycle they are every time, when they make their ship acquisition decisions. Indeed, scrap prices, combined with demand for seaborne trade and freight rates in a particular time period, shall determine whether ship owners shall consider as more optimum or not to continue operating older vessels, instead of selling them for scrap. If demand for seaborne trade at that period is high, accompanied by higher freight rates and low scrap prices, then ship owners may choose to maintain the size of their fleet with their existing vessels, or even increase it with second-hand vessels, which shall be soon delivered and put into operation (Galley, 2014). In contrast, in periods when scrap prices and demand for seaborne trade and freight rates are low, ship owners may consider as more beneficial for them to sell their older ships for scrap and invest in the acquisition of newer and more efficient vessels, which in turn shall give them the ability to benefit from high demand for seaborne trade probably at a next stage of the shipping cycle, when the newbuilding shall also have been delivered (Kagkarakis, Merikas & Merika, 2016).

3. Methodology

3.1. Research Philosophy

The research philosophy of positivism was occupied for the purposes of this research study. According to this research philosophy, there is one and only truth and it is the one that it is actually observed, without taking into account the overall social or other setting in which they are observed, as well as human feelings and emotions, which may have influenced research findings (Bryman & Bell, 2014). This research philosophy was selected, because the aim of the research study was not to interpret research results on the basis of social or other settings, but rather to comment on them as they are observed and collected.

3.2. Research Design

The research design that was occupied for the purposes of this research study was that of descriptive research. This type of research design, which is consistent with the philosophical paradigm of positivism, thereby leading to its selection, implies that research subjects are observed and studied as they are, without changing the context of their observation (Nassaji, 2015). At the same time, descriptive research is appropriate for testing research subjects that are well-defined and well-studied (Creswell,

2015). The subject of examining the factors that determine the price of vessels is a well-studied subject, forming the second reason for which descriptive research design was selected for the proposed study.

3.3.   Research Type and Strategy

Secondary research was held for the purposes of the research held in the context of this study. This type of research involves collecting and analyzing already published data from secondary sources, such as databases, academic books and journals, web sources, magazines, newspapers and other secondary sources (Treadwell, 2016). The data was quantitative, which corresponds to conducting quantitative research, the term referring to collecting and statistically analyzing data that is measurable and quantifiable. Quantitative research is appropriate, when the aim of research is to produce findings from large samples, which offer the ability to provide generalized conclusions about a subject under research, thereby leading to findings and conclusions that are more objective and reliable (Babbie, 2010). The above are the main reasons for which quantitative data was selected.

3.4.   Research Approach

The deductive research approach is the research approach that was selected for the purposes of this research study. This is the approach whereby researchers form research hypotheses and then test them with respect to existing theory and previous research findings (Sik, 2015). The above forms the aim of the research study, unlike the inductive approach, which is used for researchers that conduct research, in order to develop new theory, based on research findings. Indeed, the theory regarding prices of newbuilding and the factors determining them is an existing theory, so the aim of this research was to test the validity and reliability of this theory in the case of VLCCs.

3.5.   Data Collection and Analysis

Historical quantitative data was collected from Clarksons Shipping Intelligence Network (SIN) for the time period 2000-2018 about factors that academic literature defines as factors that could influence prices of newbuilding vessels in general and newbuilding VLCCs in specific, namely prices of second –hand vessels, earnings of VLCCs, sales in the sector, deadweight (DWT), scrap prices and freight rates (see Appendix). Statistical analysis of the data collected was held with Statistical Package for the Social Sciences (SPSS). More specifically, descriptive statistics for each of the abovementioned variables were calculated, namely means, standard deviations, minimum and maximum values for each data set. Apart from that, multiple regression analysis was held, which is appropriate for testing whether changes in more than one independent variable can predict changes in one dependent variable (Stulp & Sigaud, 2015). In the case of this research study, the dependent variable was prices of newbuilding VLCCs, while the independent variables were the abovementioned factors that are perceived as factors that influence prices of vessels in general.

Chapter 3
RESEARCH RESULTS

4.1. Descriptive Statistics of Research Variables

Taking the price of new built VLCCs first into consideration, as shown in Figure 1, prices were increasing after 2002 and until 2008. Then, a significant drop was observed in 2009. After that point in time, the price of new-built VLCCs has been declining, with a slight increase being observed from 2017 to 2018. Using the information provided in Table 1, ship owners needed on average $99.11 million during the review period, in order acquire a new VLCC. The lowest price was observed in 2002, when it cost $63.50 million to acquire a new VLCC, while at the peak of the review period in 2008 the corresponding cost reached $150 million.

Figure 1: Newbuilding Prices

Figure 2 presents how second-hand ships' prices have developed throughout the period 2000-2018. Overall, prices of second hand vessels followed the path of prices of newbuilding VLCCs over the review period. Indeed, second-hand VLCC prices kept on increasing after 2002, to reach their peak in 2007 ($135 million), before starting falling after 2007. The lowest price was observed in 2002 ($54 million). It is also important to note that in contrast to new-built VLCCs, the prices of second-hand ones fluctuated to a bigger extent after 2010. It is also worth noting that in 2014 and 2015, the price of second hand VLCCs increased, a trend that was not identified in the case of newbuilding ones. On average, ship owners over the review period needed to invest on average $80.05 million, in order to acquire a second-hand VLCC.

Figure 2: Second Hand Vessel Prices

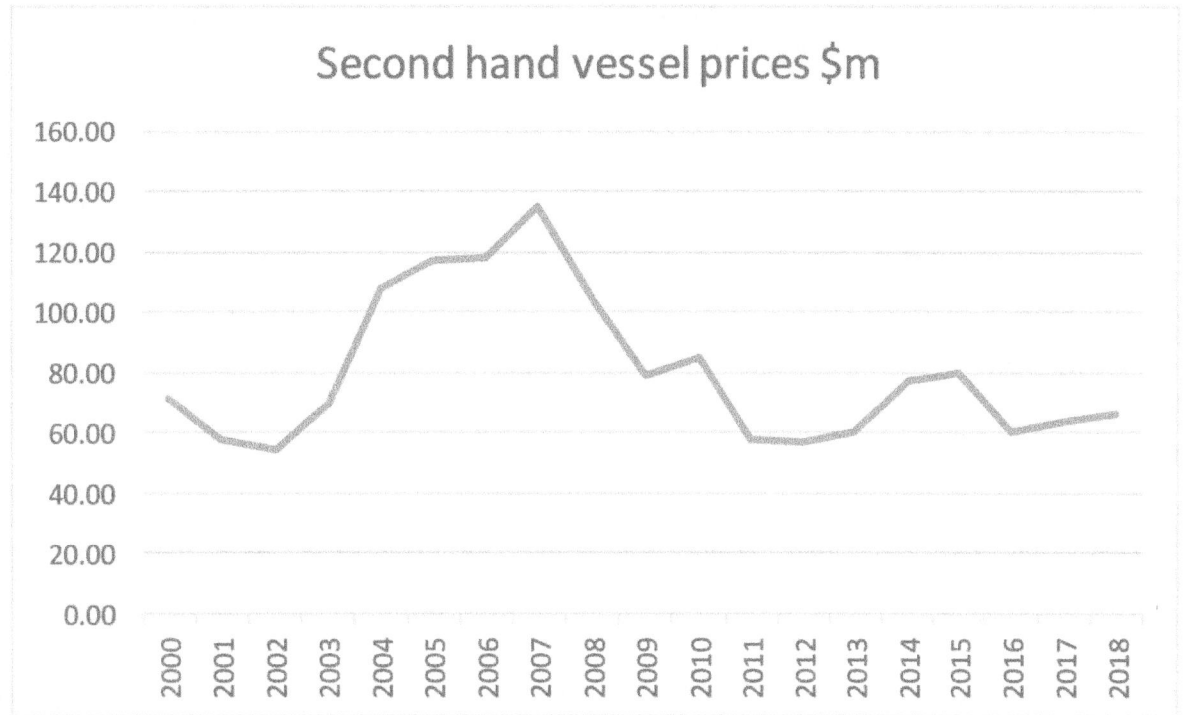

Figure 3 shows how earnings per day have developed for the case of VLCCs over the review period. The first impression that someone can get by looking at Figure 3 is that earnings per day for VLCCs were significantly fluctuated over the review period. Reaching their peak in 2007, when they earned $98,323.35 per day, ship owners of VLCCs saw their revenues reaching their lowest point in the review period in the end of the period in 2018, reaching $15,560.56. On average, owners of VLCCs earned on average $44,303.23.

Figure 3: Earnings per day

Figure 4 illustrates the development of world's seaborne trade over the period 2000-2018, which actually presents demand for seaborne trade over the review period, where VLCCs were involved in transportation. As the corresponding figure shows, demand for seaborne trade in a global context was steadily increasing from 2008 to 2008, with a slight fluctuation being observed in 2009, when demand slightly fell, before it starts increasing again from 2010 and on. 11.83 billion tons of goods and commodities were sold in 2018, up from 6.3 billion tons in 2000. On average, 1.77 billion tons of goods and commodities were sold every year during the review period.

Figure 4: Demand for Seaborne Trade

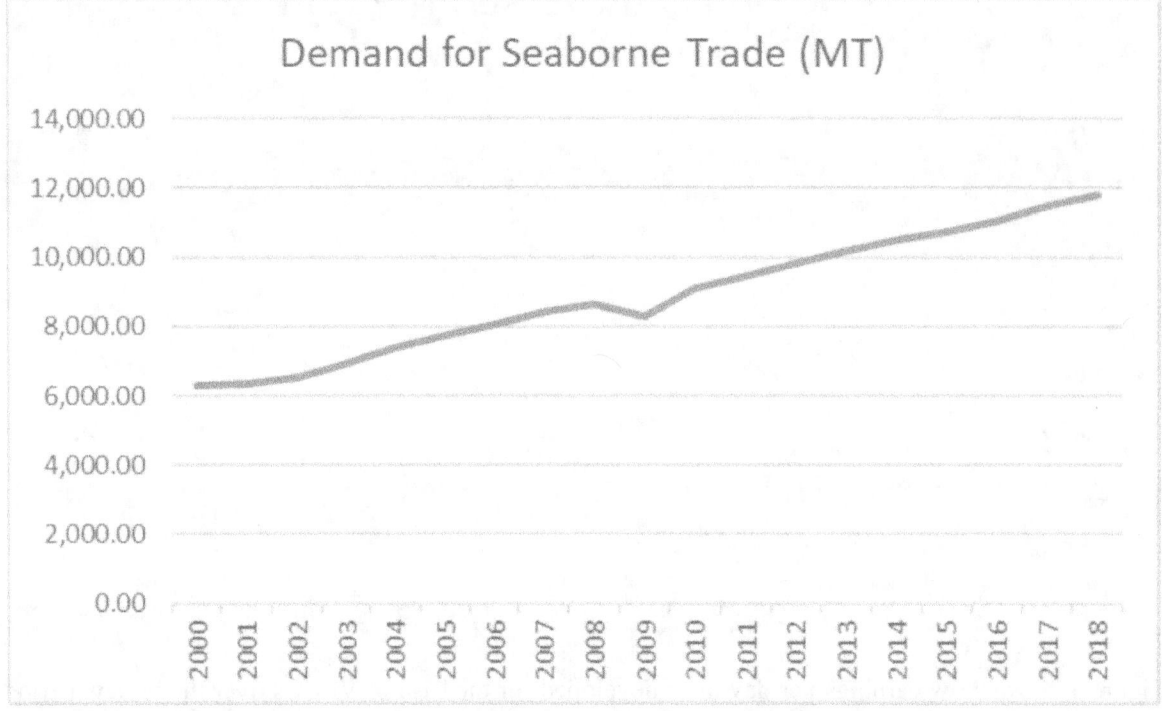

Figure 5 shows the supply of VLCCs over the review period, as measured in million DWT. Following the path of demand, supply of VLCCs was also steadily increasing from 2000 to 2018, moving from the lowest point of 123.39 million DWT in 2000 to the highest point of 226.02 million DWT in 2018 (average supply of 160.59 million DWT).

Figure 5: Vessel Supply DWT (million)

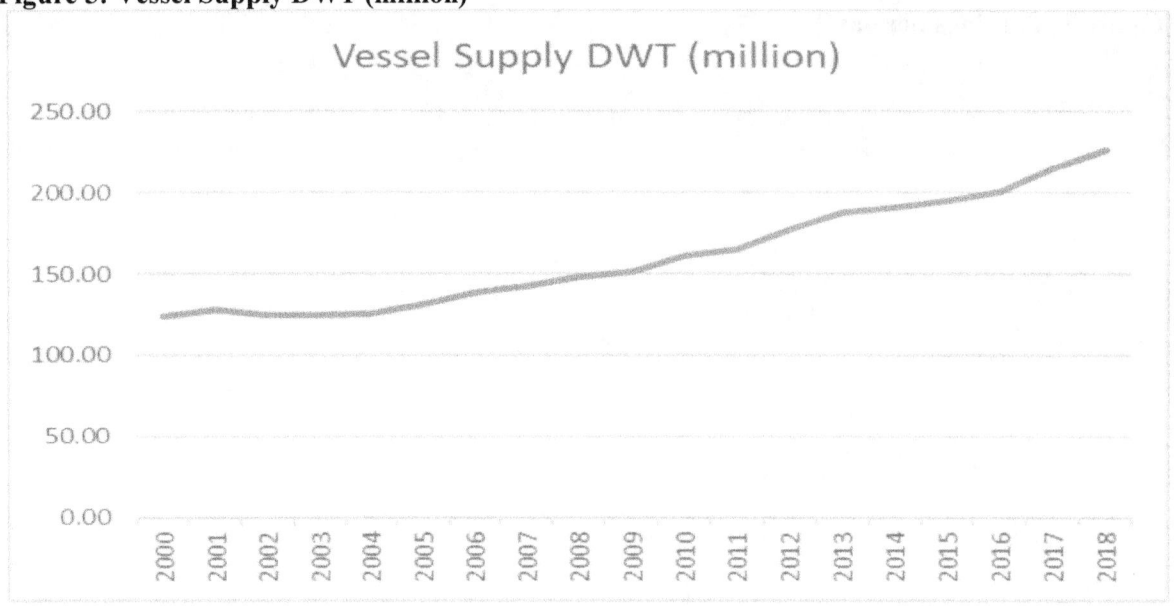

The next factor that was tested as one of the potential determinants of the price of new-built VLCCs over the review period was scrap prices, measured as $/ldt. As shown in Figure 6, the scrap price at which VLCC were sold during the review period fluctuated to a considerable extent. In particular, scrap prices for VLCCs reached their peak in 2010, when they reached $490/ldt, before starting falling until 2016. After a short increase in 2017, VLCC scrap prices fell again in 2018. The lowest point of the period was 2001, when VLCC scrap prices were $126/ldt. On average, VLCC scrap prices were $308.71/ldt.

Figure 6: Scrap Prices

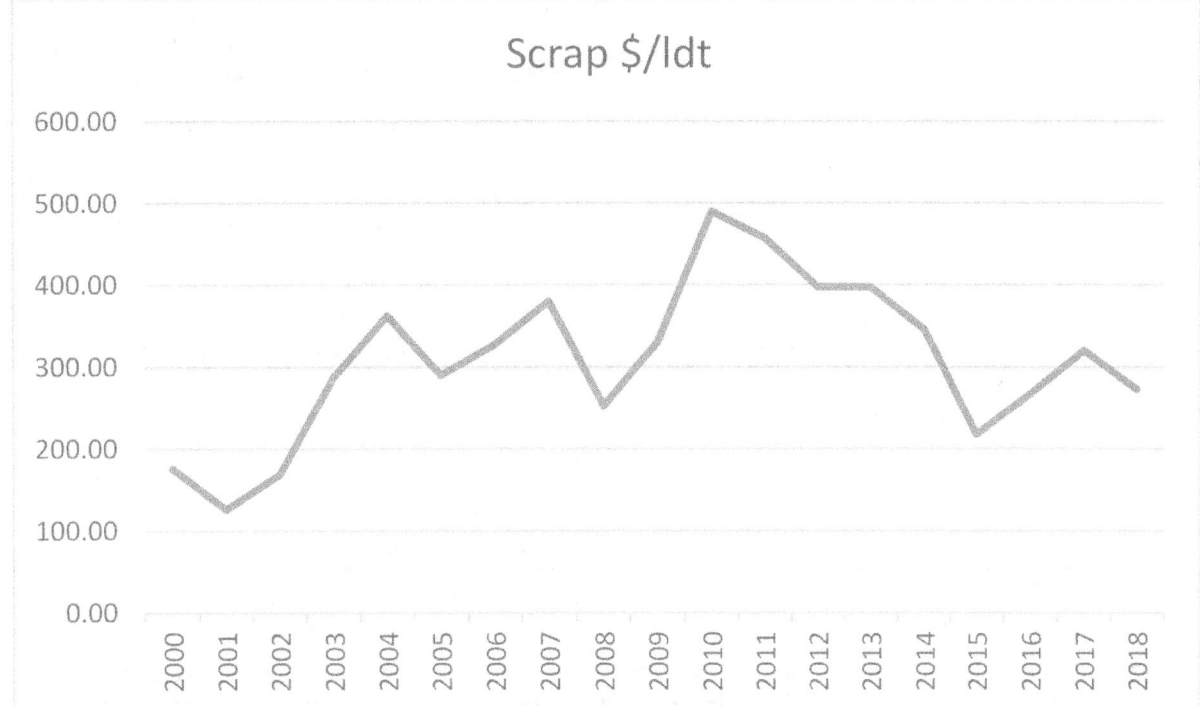

The last factor that was tested in terms of its influence on the price of new-built VLCCs during the period 2000-2018 was freight rates, measured as $/day. As illustrated in Figure 7, freight rates also fluctuated considerably during the review period. In particular, after dropping in 2002, freight rates started increasing, reaching its peak in 2008 at $73,413. Then, freight rates significantly dropped until 2013, when they reached the bottom point of the period of $19,836.54. On average, freight rates of VLCCs were $39,639.09 per day over the review period.

Figure 7: Freight Rates ($/day)

Table 1 provides a summary of the descriptive statistics that were calculated for the seven variables that were analyzed in the study:

Table 1: Descriptive Statistics

	Newbuilding $m	Second hand $m	Earnings per day $	Sales trade MT	Supply DWT million	Scrap $/ldt	Freight $/day
Mean	99.11	80.05	44,303.23	8,884.60	160.59	308.71	39,639.09
St.Dev	23.64	24.54	25,536.73	1,773.05	33.41	96.30	15,209.61
Min	63.50	54.00	15,560.56	6,311.69	123.39	126.00	19,836.54
Max	150.00	135.00	98,323.35	11,823.48	226.02	490.00	73,413.46

4.2. Regression Analysis

The results of the regression analysis that was held, in order to identify which of the independent variables of the model influenced prices of newbuilding VLCCs over the review period are presented in the following tables:

Table 2: Model Summary

Model Summary

Model	R	R Square	Adjusted R Square	Std. Error of the Estimate	Change Statistics				
					R Square Change	F Change	df1	df2	Sig. F Change
1	.943[a]	.890	.835	9.60142	.890	16.183	6	12	.000

a. Predictors: (Constant), Freight_rate, Scrap_prices, Seaborne_trade, Secondhand_prices, Earnings_per_day, Supply_DWT

Based on the model summary available at Table 2, the regression model that was developed, in order to predict the dependent variable, i.e. price of newbuilding. in fact, the R square value of the model was 0.890, which indicates a high predictive power of the regression model regarding its ability to predict the dependent variable. In fact, the model shows that changes in the independent variables of the study, namely prices of second –hand vessels, earnings of VLCCs, sales in the sector, deadweight (DWT), scrap prices and freight rates, can predict 89% of changes in the dependent variable i.e. price of new-built VLCC.

Table 3: ANOVA

ANOVA[a]

Model		Sum of Squares	df	Mean Square	F	Sig.
1	Regression	8951.042	6	1491.840	16.183	.000[b]
	Residual	1106.247	12	92.187		
	Total	10057.289	18			

a. Dependent Variable: Newbuilding_prices

b. Predictors: (Constant), Freight_rate, Scrap_prices, Seaborne_trade, Secondhand_prices, Earnings_per_day, Supply_DWT

Table 3 is the ANOVA table regarding the regression analysis that was held. Based on this table, the independent variables from which the regression model is comprised predicts the dependent variable at a statistically significant extent. The result of the regression analysis could be summarized as follows: $F_{(6,12)} = 16.183$, $p < 0.05$.

Table 4: Coefficients

Coefficients^a

Model		Unstandardized Coefficients		Standardized Coefficients	t	Sig.
		B	Std. Error	Beta		
1	(Constant)	-6.913	25.722		-.269	.793
	Secondhand_prices	.327	.213	.340	1.538	.150
	Earnings_per_day	.000	.000	-.315	-1.282	.224
	Seaborne_trade	.011	.014	.849	.829	.423
	Supply_DWT	-.467	.742	-.661	-.630	.541
	Scrap_prices	.064	.049	.259	1.296	.219
	Freight_rate	.001	.001	.772	2.266	.043

a. Dependent Variable: Newbuilding_prices

As reflected from Table 4, the coefficients table, all independent variables that were used in the regression model strongly predicted the dependent variable. From all these variables, demand for seaborne trade and supply of vessels were found to have the least influence on prices of newbuilding VLCC.

Chapter 4

DISCUSSION OF
RESEARCH RESULTS

With respect to descriptive statistics first, taking prices of new-built VLCCs first into consideration, it seems that the year 2008 has been a turning point with respect to the price performance of this vessels, with prices significantly dropping after then and never coming back to the pre-2008 levels. That the year 2008 was a turning point during the review period shall be explained by the fact that the years 2008 and 2009 were the years when the global economic crisis hit the world, after the collapse of the U.S. real estate market and its domino effects in a global context. It seems that the effects of the global economic crisis on an industry of global magnitude, as the shipping industry is, were so sharp that led to the collapse of the prices of new vessels; having to face so many adverse economic conditions, ship owners would not be able to invest in the acquisition of new vessels, unless shipyards decided to reduce their prices.

The same was the case with the prices of second-hand vessels, initially verifying the relationship between the prices of newbuilding and second-hand vessels. Under no doubt, it was more than obvious that from the moment that prices of new-built VLCCs fell after 2008, the same would also happen with the price of second-hand VLCCs as well, in order for the difference between the two to maintained. Otherwise, ship owners would no longer have the incentive to invest in the acquisition of new vessels. After all, as it was shown in Table 1 in the previous section, the prices of newbuilding and second-hand VLCCs was not so much different during the review period. In other words, unless ship owners' decision was based on efficiency and other factors than price, they must have been marginal in their decisions to purchase new or second-hand VLCCs. This also shows how important VLCCs are for ship owners and the shipping industry in general; even if second-hand, it seems that VLCCs do not lose their value over time, obviously thanks to the important advantages they offer to ship owners, as these were analyzed by Cullinane & Khanna (2000) and Zrinc et al. (2006).

The third variable that was analyzed in this study was earnings per day for the case of VLCCs over the period 2000-2018. The analysis held in the previous section indicated that VLCC owners enjoyed two peaks over the review period, one in 2004 and one in 2008. After 2008, a significant drop in ship owners' earnings was reported, probably as one more consequence of the global economic crisis, which led to the collapse of prices of new and second-hand vessels as well. Obviously, knowing that the earnings of VLCC owners had collapsed, shipyards could do nothing else but reduce their offered prices for new ships. The collapse in the earnings of VLCCs' owners shall be definitely attributed to the tragic effects of the global economic crisis of 2009 on the economics of shipping companies, as well as the decisions that ship owners had to make, in order to survive. Indeed, as analyzed previously, following the discussion by Sanchez & Pérez Salas (2009), as well as that by Hung & Chuang (2012), at the start of the crisis freight rates collapsed by 85%, with the result that ship owners could not even cover their operating costs. It seems, however, that the global economic crisis must not have been the only factor negatively influencing VLCCs owners' earnings over the review period. Both in 2002 and later on in 2018 the earnings of VLCC owners were lower than those in 2009. It follows from the above that VLCC owners have faced difficult times over the review period, not necessarily because of the global economic crisis.

With respect to global seaborne trade with regards to VLCCs, this research indicated that demand for shipping services offered by VLCCs have been increasing since 2000, at least until 2018, which is the last year of the review period. Under no doubt, this is a very positive and promising performance for the VLCC sector. On the other hand, though, it is highly problematic that in a period of constantly rising demand for seaborne trade, VLCC owners have experienced such fluctuations in their earnings. At the same time, it becomes evident that demand for seaborne trade is certainly not the only factors shaping the dynamics of the shipping industry, both in general and as far as prices of new and second-hand vessels is concerned.

Supply of VLCCs was also found to have been increasing from 2000 to 2018. This was a clear indication from research findings that the traditional relationships between supply and demand has been verified in the case of the VLCC shipping sector. As obvious, increasing demand for VLCC seaborne trade has been associated with increasing supply, which shall be attributed to ship owners placing orders for new ships, as a means of anticipating the additional needs for vessels for ship owners to take advantage of increasing demand. The above totally verified the basic shipping theory provided by Stopford (2009), based on which, when demand for seaborne trade is high, ship owners tend to order more vessels, in order to benefit for this increase in demand. Such a finding somehow contradicts the analysis held in Chapter 2 regarding the consequence of the global economic crisis. Indeed, as analyzed earlier in this research study, several ship owners began to withdraw their ships from the market and others scaled back to very large extent their investments in new shipyards only in the first months from the start of the crisis in mid-2008. It was also analyzed that the year 2012 was a year characterized by a reduced number of new orders and a large number of cancellations of vessel deliveries. The above could mean that although these were the characteristics of the global shipping industry overall, the case was not the same in the more particular case of the VLCC sector, where supply of new vessels was steadily increasing in 2008 and on, up until at least 2018, the last year of the review period. It seems that even when ship owners had to stope operating some vessels and cancelled the building or delivery of some others, they did not do the same with the VLCCs they had ordered, probably seeing at these megaships the solution to decreasing their operating costs, instead of keeping on operating less efficient and smaller ships.

If regression analysis had not been held, someone could argue that another basic shipping theory provided by Stopford (2009) was not verified by research findings, the one whereby in periods of high demand for vessels, their price increases, since ship owners are willing to pay more to acquire vessels that will help them in increasing their sales potential. As it was analyzed before, although demand for seaborne trade was constantly increasing since 2000, after 2008 prices of ships did not increase, but actually decreased. Of course, the above is a basic theory, which does not take into account periods of crises, like the global economic crisis, whose development was fully encompassed in the time period under review. During that period, ship owners continued to order new VLCCs, but at lower prices than before. This means that increasing demand may be a factor that could lead to increasing prices of vessels, but this is not the only factor determining prices. Further to that, although research findings indicated that increasing demand was accompanied by increasing supply of VLCCs during the review period, they do not show whether supply was adequate enough to anticipate the total of increasing demand, while they also did not indicate whether demand for and earnings of VLCCs were such that would give the ability to the shipping market and ship owners to absorb high prices of VLCCs, either new or second-hand ones.

As far as scrap prices are concerned, Chapter 2 presented two somehow opposing theories regarding how scrap prices could influence prices of vessels. The first was the one outlined by Stopford (2009), based on which, when scrap prices are high, ship owners find it more attractive to demolish their older ships and purchase new ones, this increase in demand also leading to increase in prices of new vessels (Stopford, 2009). The other is that of Galley (2014), based on which it is the stage of the life cycle that shall determine the influence that scrap prices may have in prices of new and second-hand vessels. Under this theory, if demand for seaborne trade is high, and scrap prices are low, then ship owners may choose to maintain the size of their fleet with their existing vessels, or even increase it with second-hand vessels, which shall be soon delivered and put into operation. Based on the findings of the research held for the purposes of this research study, when demand for VLCC-related seaborne trade was rising from 2000 to 2008, so did supply of VLCCs and at that time scrap prices were increasing, while so did prices of both new and second hand VLCCs. After 2008, while supply and demand of VLCCs kept on rising, scrap prices were falling and so were doing prices of new and second hand vessels. It becomes evident from the above that prices of newbuilding VLCCs in the review period more or less followed the path of scrap prices, without, however, following exactly the ups and downs of scrap prices over the review period and especially after 2010. Once again, the above indicate how many factors shall influence prices of vessels in the VLCC sector, as this is also evident in existing academic literature for all types of vessels, after all.

The last factor that was tested in terms of its influence on the price of new-built VLCCs during the period 2000-2018 was freight rates. As the findings of the research indicated, freight rates also fluctuated considerably during the review period. In particular, after dropping in 2002, freight rates started increasing, reaching their peak in 2008, before starting dropping. These findings indicate that prices of new and second hand VLCCs have gone almost hand by hand with freight rates, which is a relationship verifying the respective analysis of Cullinane (2011). What was not verified, though, was the direct relationship between freight rates and ship owners' earnings, as well as between freight rates and supply of vessels. Indeed, as the corresponding figures and descriptive statistics indicate, although there were years during the review period when freight rates were high, earnings per day were not so high for ship owners in the same years. At the same time, although freight rates significantly fluctuated over the review period, supply of VLCCs kept on increasing on a steady pace. One explanation for this phenomenon may come from the findings of Kou & Luo (2015), based on which ship owners take their ship acquisition decisions for newbuilding not based on freight rates in the short-run, but rather freight rates' forecast for the long-run. Obviously, from the moment that demand for seaborne trade in the sector was constantly, as well as from the moment that freight rates fluctuated, VLCC owners may have decided to continue placing orders to expand their fleet, hoping that increasing demand would sometime lead to also increasing freight rates, at least as it did from 2000 to 2008.

With respect to earnings, it has been indeed surprising that VLCC owners did not enjoy earnings equivalent with freight rates. This indicates that apart from general market rules, there are also other, sector or even company-specific factors, which may negatively influence ship-owners' earnings, even in periods when freight rates are high. As far as newbuilding prices are concerned, Kou & Luo (2015) found that they are more elastic to long-run forecasts and fluctuations of freight rates. In the above context, taking the research findings into consideration, it becomes evident that prices of newbuilding VLCCs have not exactly followed the path of freight rates. In fact, the general rule that high freight rates are associated with high prices of vessels has been verified by research findings. However, the findings also showed that it takes time for prices of newbuilding (and second-hand vessels) to adjust to fluctuations in freight rates.

At the core of interest of this research study was to identify whether the factors that were analyzed before influence prices of new VLCCs. The response to this core research question was provided by the results of the regression analysis that was held, based on which the regression model that was developed with all these variables statistically significantly predicted changes in prices of newbuilding VLCCs. These results verify to a big extent the academic framework on which this study was based, as outlined in the literature review chapter. Indeed, those factors that academic literature and previous research findings have found to influence prices of new and second hand vessels in general were those factors that were also found to influence prices of new-built VLCCs over the time period 2000-2018. Taking into consideration that six independent variables were used in the regression model as factors that could potentially influence prices of new VLCCs, the findings of the research show the multidimensional and complex nature of ship prices, as well as other factors encompassed in the complex and challenging business of shipping companies.

As derived from the analysis of the coefficients table that was produced, although the regression model that was developed significantly predicted the dependent variable, there were two factors that were found not to contribute to the prediction of changes to prices of newly-built VLCCs to the extent that the other factors did. These two factors were demand for seaborne trade and supply of vessels, which were found to have the least influence on prices of newbuilding VLCCs. Based on the findings of the research, as well the fundamental assumptions of maritime economics theory, as developed in Chapter 2, this was a somehow surprising outcome, in the sense that not only in the shipping industry, but also in any other industry, demand and supply are the two out of the three basic components of basic economic models, the third being price. Of course, this does not mean that research findings did not verify the above axiom, since demand and supply were indeed found to influence prices of newbuilding, but not to the same extent as other factors. It seems that at least for the review period and at least for the particular case of the VLCC sector, there may have been other factors that have been more important than demand and supply in influencing the prices of newbuilding VLCCs, such as scrap prices, earnings, freight rates and second-hand vessel prices, i.e. the other factors that were used in the analysis as independent variables. It also seems that demand for seaborne trade has influenced ship owners' decisions to order new vessels and not the price at which such orders shall be placed. After all, based on the fundamental maritime economics theory provided by Stopford (2009), when demand for seaborne trade is high, ship owners tend to order more vessels, in order to benefit for this increase in demand. In such periods of high demand for vessels, their price increases, since ship owners are willing to pay more to acquire vessels that will help them in increasing their sales potential. It follows from the above that if ship owners believe there is strong potential to increase their sales, and of they believe that the acquisition of new vessels shall offer important benefits to them, they shall order new vessels at any cost. This is a mechanism that probably explains why prices of vessels increase in periods of high demand. Obviously, in periods of high demand, ship builders have the knowledge and experience to know and expect the reactions of ship owners in terms of their wish to acquire new and more efficient vessels the soonest possible, so they know that they can raise their prices, since increased prices shall not prevent ship owners from placing their orders soon.

If the academic framework developed in Chapter 2 is taken into account, then, if the coefficients table was to exclude some factors from those having a great influence in price of newbuilding, this would be earnings per day. Indeed, based on the analysis of Cullinane (2011), when freight rates are high, earnings of vessels are also high, which adds to the willingness of ship owners to expand their fleet to gain higher revenues, thereby again creating higher demand for vessels, which in turn increases their prices. However, in the case of this research study, as also analyzed above, earnings per day did not exactly follow the path of freight rates. As such, it once again becomes evident that even of earnings of ships owners were not as expected, based on the performance of freight rates, prices of new VLCCs, kept on increasing, obviously reflecting increasing demand and the numerous benefits that megaships offer to ship owners, as these have been widely analyzed in this research study.

As a last point, one of the main objectives of this research study was also to comment on whether the fact that many VLCC have been scrapped shall be attributed to any of the factors considering supply, demand and prices of such vessels, or only to the fact that they tend to be substituted with ULCCs. First of all, it is worth noting that if the analysis of Maritime Executive (2021) is taken into consideration, while ship owners are in general keen on demolishing their older and smaller ships, in order to purchase newer, more efficient and larger ones, this has not been a trend after 2021. Indeed, while ship owners could demolish their older VLCCs to purchase new ULCCs, they have instead decided to maintain their older VLCCs for two main reasons. The first is is that VLCCs offer ship owners high earnings and profits potential, while the second is the high prices of second-hand vessels, which has given the incentive to owners of older VLCCs to sell them in the second-hand market, rather than abolish them and sell them for scrap. Of course, the above trends refer to the period after 2021, which was a period characterized by the huge economic consequences of the COVID-19 pandemic. Before 2021, the trend of abolishing older VLCCs was more often. The above indicate that ship owners' decisions for demolishing their VLCCs are the same factors that influence the price of such new vessels, i.e. supply, demand and price of second-hand vessels at most, with the exception here being scrap prices, which ship owners take into account only when supply, demand and prices of vessels are such that could make it more beneficial for them to demolish their older ships, rather than maintaining them in their fleet or selling them for scrap. In any case, the fact that VLCC owners have decided to stop demolishing so many of their ships shall also be attributed to the disadvantages of megaships, as these have been analyzed by Cariou (2008), as well as Chen & Zhang (2008). Indeed, the fact that megaships cannot pass through some major sea passages, as well as that they are difficult to navigate and more expensive to acquire and operate, may have been additional factors for which ship owners of VLCCs may have decided not to demolish so many of their older VLCCs, as they did in the past.

Chapter 5
CONCLUSION

The aim of this research study was to identify and analyze the determinants of prices of newbuilding vessels in the Very Large Crude Carriers (VLCC) Sector. More specifically, this research study had the following objectives:

- To identify the factors that determine the prices of newbuilding vessels in the VLCC sector
- To examine whether these factors are consistent with those that academic literature suggests as factors that determine the price of newbuilding vessels in the shipping industry in general
- To comment on whether the fact that many VLCC have been scrapped shall be attributed to any of the factors considering supply, demand and prices of such vessels, or only to the fact that they tend to be substituted with ULCCs
- To provide implications for ship owners, as far as their vessel-acquisition decisions for VLCC are concerned

Based on the findings of the research, prices of new built VLCCs were increasing after 2002 and until 2008. Then, a significant drop was observed in 2009. After that point in time, the price of new-built VLCCs has been declining, with a slight increase being observed from 2017 to 2018. Prices of second hand vessels followed the path of prices of newbuilding VLCCs over the review period, while it is worth noting that in 2014 and 2015, the price of second hand VLCCs increased, a trend that was not identified in the case of newbuilding ones. Earnings per day for VLCCs were significantly fluctuated over the review period. Ship owners of VLCCs saw their revenues reaching their lowest point in the review period in the end of the period in 2018. Demand for VLCC-seaborne trade in a global context was steadily increasing from 2008 to 2018, with a slight fluctuation being observed in 2009, when demand slightly fell, before it starts increasing again from 2010 and on. Following the path of demand, supply of VLCCs was also steadily increasing from 2000 to 2018. The scrap price at which VLCC were sold during the review period fluctuated to a considerable extent. Scrap prices for VLCCs reached their peak in 2010, before starting falling until 2016, while, after a short increase in 2017, VLCC scrap prices fell again in 2018. Freight rates also fluctuated considerably during the review period. In particular, after dropping in 2002, freight rates started increasing, reaching their peak in 2008, before significantly dropping until 2013.

Research findings have very important implications, both theoretical and practical ones. More specifically, also taking into consideration the aim and objectives of this research, research findings indicated that the factors that determines price of new vessels in the shipping industry in general are more or less the factors that also determine the price of new-built VLCCs as well. The above conclusion is very important for ship owners, since it gives them the ability to make their decisions on the basis of some fundamental factors and axioms that are met in the shipping industry in a global context, no matter the shipping sector their company operates in. As such, by monitoring general factors and trends in the global shipping industry, VLCCs' owners have the ability to take their informed decisions in the particular case of their sector as well.

Another important conclusion has to do with the factors that determine the price of newbuilding VLCCs. Indeed, research findings indicate that in periods of high demand for seaborne trade, they shall expect to invest more money for the acquisition of new ships, especially when supply is not adequate enough to cover the increased demand for seaborne trade in their sector. In other words, owners of VLCCs shall know that in periods of high demand, when they shall definitely wish to find ways to expand their fleet, they shall be able to do so at prices higher than in periods of lower demand. For these decisions, their earnings per day shall also contribute to an understanding of whether they shall invest in the acquisition of ships at certain prices, while their decisions shall also be influenced – at least to some extent – by scrap prices as well.

Further to the above, it is also worth commenting on the implications provided by the finding that earnings per day and freight rates do not exactly follow the same line. Under no doubt, freight rates determine ship owners' earnings. However, this does not mean that when freight rates increase, ship owners' earnings shall keep on increasing at the same pace. At the same time, though, it shall mean that prices of ships shall increase, because shipyards get the message that ship owners' earnings are about to increase and demand for seaborne trade is also increasing, so they sell their news ships that are in high demand at higher prices.

As a last point, it is also important for ship owners to also take into account the geopolitical, economic and overall conditions, trends and dynamics of the world, when making their business decisions, as well as when they try to estimate the factors that could influence prices of new – and second hand – vessels every time. Indeed, as it was widely analyzed in the main part of this research study, the global economic crisis at most, but also the COVID-19 pandemic and the war in Ukraine were also incidents of global magnitude, which have influenced not only the global shipping industry, as well as global economy and the world overall. As already witnessed in the case of VLCCs that were examined here, such incidents and conditions in a global context could significantly alter the trends and dynamics of the global shipping industry, thereby also explaining why some factors were found to influence the price of newbuilding VLCCs more than others, merely contrasting some of the findings of previous research. It follows from the above that when ship owners make their decisions and predictions of the prices of new vessels they wish to acquire, they definitely have to anticipate the occurrence and potential effects of major global events.

Last but not least, this dissertation was subject to certain methodological limitations. Forst of all, the data collected corresponded to a period of only 19 years. Although such a period is a considerable amount of time, so that reliable conclusions about the subject under research can be drawn, if data for more years had been collected, then more in-depth insights would have been held regarding the factors that influence the price of newbuilding. Of course, this was a limitation deriving from the fact that the research study referred to the particular case of VLCCs, which are newer vessels in the market, so it was obvious that not much data would be available from this type of vessels. In this context, future researchers are recommended to conduct the same type of research with other vessel types as well, as a means of providing a better and deeper understanding regarding the factors that influence the prices of newbuilding vessels in general. Last but not least, the research held with respect to this study was secondary. Future researchers, having more adequate time and resources, could conduct primary research with shipping experts on the same subject, as a means of identifying other factors that they may take into account, when deciding on whether the price of a vessel is worth investing in her, which may not be attributed to the more common factors that are provided through academic literature.

REFERENCES

Adland, R., & Koekebakker, S. (2007). Ship Valuation Using Cross-Sectional Sales Data: A Multivariate Non-Parametric Approach. Maritime Economics & Logistics, 105-118.

Adland, R., Norland, K., & Sætrevik, E. (2017). The Impact of Shipyard and Shipowner Heterogeneity on Contracting Prices in the Newbuilding Market. Maritime Business Review, 2(2), 58-78.

Babbie, E. R. (2010). The Practice of Social Research. 12th Edition. Belmont, California: Wadsworth Publishing.

Bertzeletou, M. (2022). Crude Tanker Annual Review – 2022. Available from https://www.thesignalgroup.com/newsroom/crude-tanker-annual-review-2022. Retrieved 6th January, 2023.

Branch, A. E. (2007). Elements of Shipping. Chapman & Hall Publications.

Bryman, A., & Bell, E. (2014). Business Research Methods for Business Students. 4th Edition. Harlow: Prentice Hall Publications.

Cariou, P. (2008). Serving Tomorrow's Mega Size Container Ships. International Journal Ocean Systems Management, 1.

Chen, F., & Zhang, R. (2008), Economic Viability of Mega-Size Containership in Different Service Networks. Journal Shanghai Jiaotong University, 13(2), 221-225. Creswell, J. W. (2015). A Concise Introduction to Mixed Methods Research. Sage Publications.

Cullinane, K. (2011). International Handbook of Maritime Economics. London: Edward Elgar Publications.

Cullinane, K., & Khanna, M. (2000). Economies of Scale in Large Containerships: Optimal Size and Geographical Implications. Journal of Transport Geography, 8, 181-195.

Galley, M. (2014). Shipbreaking: Hazards and Liabilities. Springer Publications.

Grammenos, C. (2013). The Handbook of Maritime Economics and Business. Taylor & Francis Publications.

Hung, C. T., & Chuang, F. C. (2012). The Influence of Global Economic Crisis towards the Financial Performance of the Shipping Industry. Applied Mechanics and Materials, 145, 480-484.

Kagkarakis, N. D., Merikas, A. G., & Merika, A. (2016). Modelling and Forecasting the Demolition Market in Shipping. Maritime Policy & Management, 43(8):1021–1035.

Karan, C. (2021). What are Very Large Crude Carrier (VLCC) and Ultra Large Crude Carrier (ULCC)? Available from https://www.marineinsight.com/types-of-ships/what-are-very-large-crude-carrier-vlcc-and-ultra-large-crude-carrier-ulcc/. Retrieved 6th January, 2023.

Kou, Y., & Luo, M. (2015). Modelling the Relationship between Ship Price and Freight Rate with Structural Changes. Journal of Transport Economics and Policy, 49(2), 276-294.

Maritime Executive (2021). VLCC Demolition at Low Levels in 2021 Despite Weak Rates. Available from https://maritime-executive.com/article/vlcc-demolition-at-low-levels-in-2021-despite-weak-rates. Retrieved 25th August, 2023.

Market Watch (2023). Crude Oil Carrier Market Opportunities, Demand and Forecasts 2023-2028 with Top Countries Data. Available from https://www.marketwatch.com/press-release/crude-oil-carrier-market-opportunities-demand-and-forecasts-2023-2028-with-top-countries-data-2023-01-02. Retrieved 6th January, 2023.

Michail, N. A. (2000). World Economic Growth and Seaborne Trade Volume: Quantifying the Relationship. Transportation Research Interdisciplinary Perspectives, 4.

Nassaji, H. (2015). Qualitative and Descriptive Research: Data Type versus Data Analysis. Language Teaching Research, 19(2), 129-132.

Sanchez, R. J., & Pérez Salas, G. (2009). The Economic Crisis and the Maritime and Port Sector. Available from https://repositorio.cepal.org/bitstream/handle/11362/36278/1/FAL_271_economic_crisis_en.pdf. Retrieved 26th August, 2023.

Sik, K. (2015). Tradition or Modernism in Grammar Teaching: Deductive vs. Inductive Approaches. Procedia - Social and Behavioral Sciences, 197, 2141 – 2144.

Stopford, M. (2009). Maritime Economics. 3rd Edition. Routledge Publications.

Stulp, F., & Sigaud, O. (2015). Many Regression Algorithms, One Unified Model: A Review. Neural Networks, 69, 60–79.

Tai, H. H., & Wang, Y. M. (2022). Influence of Vessel Upsizing on Pollution Emissions along Far East–Europe Trunk Routes. Environmental Science & Pollution Research, 29, 65322–65333.

Talley, W. K. (2012). Blackwell Companion to Maritime Economics. UK: John Wiley and Sons Ltd.

Treadwell, D. F. (2016). Introducing Communication Research: Paths of Inquiry. Thousand Oaks, CA: SAGE Publications.

Zrinc, N., Oguamanam, D., Bosnjak, S. (2006). Dynamic and Modelling of Mega Quayside Container Cranes. Faculty of Mechanical Engineering Transactions, 34, 193-198.

APPENDIX
Research Data

DATE	NEWBUILDING $M	SECOND HAND $M	EARNINGS PER DAY $	SALES TRADE MT	SUPPLY DWT MILLION	SCRAP $/LDT	FREIGHT $/DAY
2000	76.50	71.00	55,440	6,311.69	123.39	175.50	43,650
2001	70.00	58.00	38,829	6,354.76	128.00	126.00	40,490
2002	63.50	54.00	23,293	6,539.65	124.38	169.00	25,824
2003	77.00	70.00	52,453	6,915.12	124.58	287.50	34,260
2004	110.00	108.00	98,323	7,370.16	125.17	362.50	55,557
2005	120.00	117.00	62,558	7,735.48	131.23	290.00	58,529
2006	129.00	118.00	64,914	8,053.58	138.16	327.50	58,308
2007	146.00	135.00	58,795	8,434.94	142.19	380.00	55,548
2008	150.00	104.00	97,152	8,632.07	147.68	252.50	73,413
2009	101.00	79.00	28,434	8,276.45	150.96	330.00	39,577
2010	105.00	85.00	33,797	9,084.23	160.53	490.00	37,962
2011	99.00	58.00	18,263	9,459.74	164.72	457.50	24,947
2012	93.00	57.00	21,187	9,834.28	176.91	397.50	22,125
2013	94.00	60.00	18,621	10,168.11	187.47	397.50	19,837
2014	97.00	77.00	30,015	10,505.51	190.45	345.00	28,115
2015	93.50	80.00	64,846	10,734.68	194.52	217.50	48,433
2016	84.50	60.00	41,488	11,061.53	200.25	267.50	36,585
2017	81.50	64.00	17,794	11,511.95	214.66	320.00	27,084
2018	92.50	66.00	15,561	11,823.48	226.02	272.50	22,899

www.ingramcontent.com/pod-product-compliance
Lightning Source LLC
Chambersburg PA
CBHW080002130626
46546CB00014B/2800